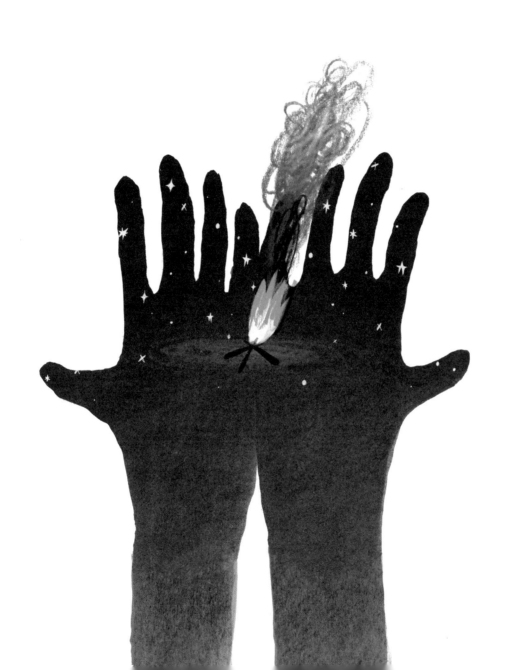

Tell me, what is it you plan to do
with your one wild and precious life?

— Mary Oliver, "The Summer Day," *House of Light*, 1990

To Arn,
my advisor, fellow navigator, and friend
who helped me gather this book out of
the chaos of my mind.

OLIVER JEFFERS

BEGIN AGAIN

PHILOMEL

WHERE

with FIRE

I suppose.

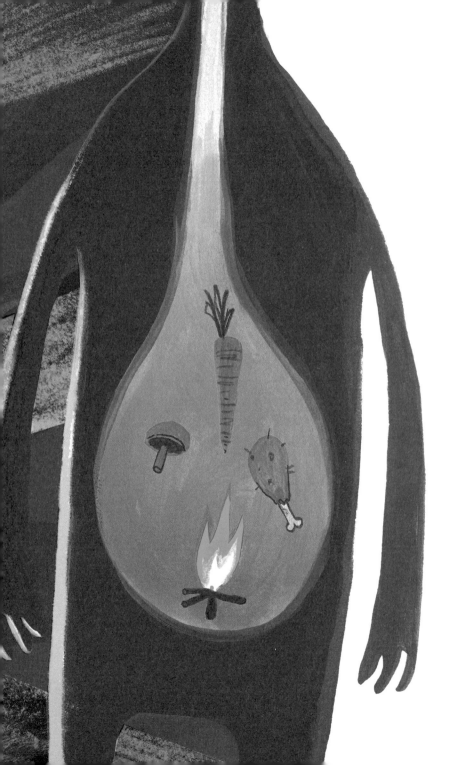

IT MOVED US
UP the LADDER

FREED the
ENERGY
from OUR
BELLIES   to...

OUR BRAINS that WOULD CREATE WORDS

SEE PATTERNS

Tell STORIES

Invent the FUTURE.

NO. WAIT.

WE BEGAN BEFORE THAT.

WE BEGAN with OUR HANDS

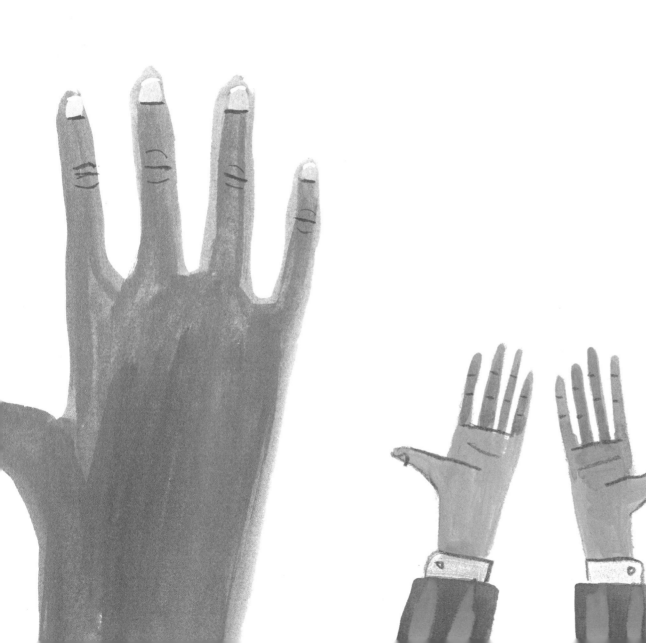

(we needed to light those fires somehow!)

WE picked up DEBRIS, put it
TOGEther and MADE TOOLS

A STICK and a STONE
Bound to each other
BECAME A HAMMER.

somewhere along the Road came

A Wheel...   A Drill...

A Phone ...

A SPACE ROCKET.

WE USED These Things

AT FIRST,
To simply SURVIVE.

Then to EXPLORE,

then CONTROL

and then Play.

For the FIRST Time
WE HAD TIME

Time to consider Beauty

To make For the
Pleasure of MAKing

LIVE
WITHOUT
thought of

Death.

NO. WAIT. REALLY.

WE BEGAN BEFORE EVEN THAT.

WHEN WE EMERGED ON DRY LAND

STOOD ON TWO FEET
put ONE in FRONT of the other and Kept WALKING.

IT is OUR FEET that take us
where we want to go.

BUT   WHERE   DO WE   WANT   TO GO ?

IF the PREDICTIONS
WERE TRUE,
WE'D BE LIVING
IN SPACE BY NOW.

All of US.

BEYOND the air
WE BREAthe

AND HEADING
FURTHER YET.

WE ARE STILL HERE

ON THIS DRY LAND
where WE'VE ALWAYS Been,

ON WHICH WE have NOW DRAWN
IMAGINARY LINES
SO WE KNOW

WHO WE ARE   AND WHO WE ARE NOT

US   THEM

WHERE   WE belong   and where we DO NOT

TAKING WHAT WE WANT

WHEN WE WANT IT.

The KINGS of OUR CASTLES

on our ISLANDS of ISOLATION

Admired by STRANGERS

(SAFE from those STRANGERS)

And REMEMBER
in A WORLD full of strangers

WE ALL NEED

TO COME FROM SOMEWHERE.

Though, when you LOOK From FAR ENOugh

IT IS CLEAR WE ALL come From EARth...

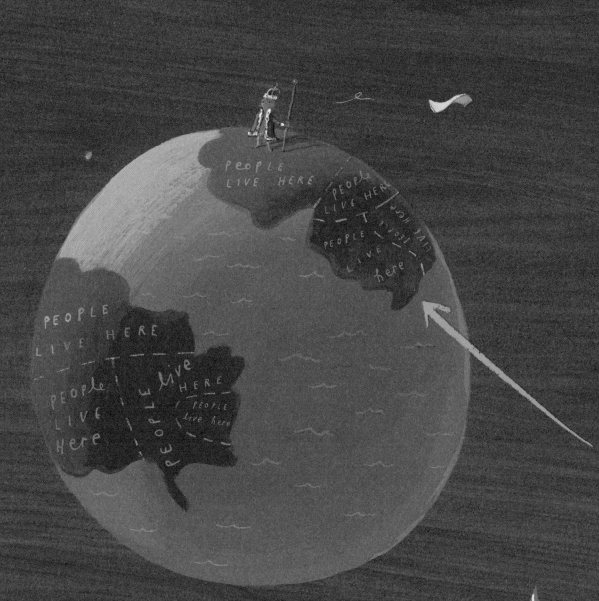

PEOPLE LIVE HERE

PEOPLE LIVE HERE

PEOPLE LIVE HERE

PEOPLE LIVE HERE

PEOPLE LIVE HERE

PEOPLE LIVE HERE

PEOPLE LIVE HERE

so there is ONLY US

ONLY EARTHLY CONTENTMENT–

After all
we are, still, simple creatures . . .

WHICH IS WHY we are
DRAWN to an OPEN Fire.
The Sound of A VIOlin
WHY WE EMBRACE the Touch
OF WOOD and WARM light

PEOPle LIKE to Feel warm

Both on the skin

and in The
Heart

RE A lly...

WHAT WE MOSTLY WANT

IS EACH OTHER

When you THINK ABOUT it
WE ENJOY giving the RIGHT THING

MORE   than   HAVING   IT.

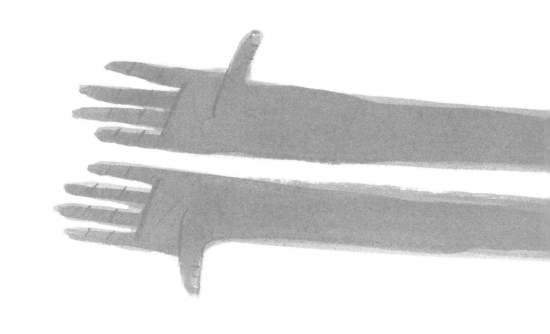

AND the FIRST thing WE DO, AFter laughing at a GOOD joke OR HEARING A GOOD STORY, is THink...

who

CAN WE TELL it to?

That's HOW IT ALWAYS WAS

the SLOW PASSING of STORIES to And For

STORIES that gave us SAFE HARBOR and an idea

EAch other

of WHERE WE FIT in The LONG line of TIME.

SOMEwhere   Along   THAT   LINE

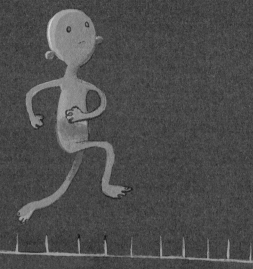

it has ALL STARTED TO SPEED UP.

The FUTURE SHORTened to the Limitations

OF OUR OWN

LIFE

This LIFE
in WHICH WE   ALONE   are CAST

IN THE STARRING ROLE.

so... where does that bring us?
SO WHERE ARE WE ALL going again?

Well...

WE DON'T KNOW WHERE

BUT IT'S A RACE NOW TO GET THERE

Feet RUNNing ONE in FRONT of the OTHER

TOWARDS EASIER, FASTER, NEWER, CHEAPER

AND AS WE RACE,

WE USE THESE SAME

HANDS

(THAT BUILT
SPACE ROCKETS)

TO   HOLD   EACH   OTHER   BACK

AND   PULL   EACH   OTHER   DOWN...

CHOOSING
TIME and Again
That it's
MORE IMPORTANT
TO BE   RIGHT
over WRONG

Than to be
BETTER
OVER WORSE.

THE DIFFERENCE BETWEEN RIGHT...

and BETTER

IS That BEING RIGHT
IS About proving the PAST

while being better is about
building the FUTURE.

WE should KNOW BY NOW...

That WHILE
IT's WISE TO keep an EYE
ON The PAST
(FoR we oFTEN repeat ouR mistakes)

IF WE KEEP BOTH EYES
on the PAST

WE ARE Blind

FOR we are not going that way.

SO, WHERE <u>ARE</u> WE going?

IS OUR CURRENT course
WORTHY of TURNING  THOUGHTS into

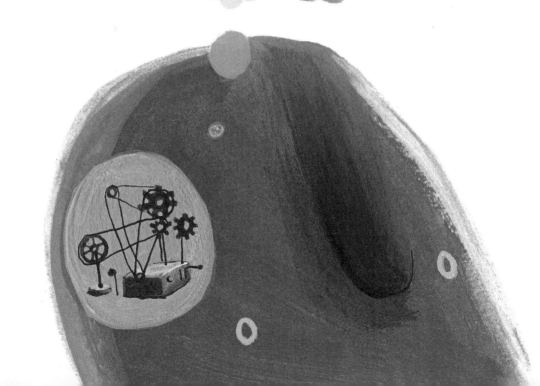

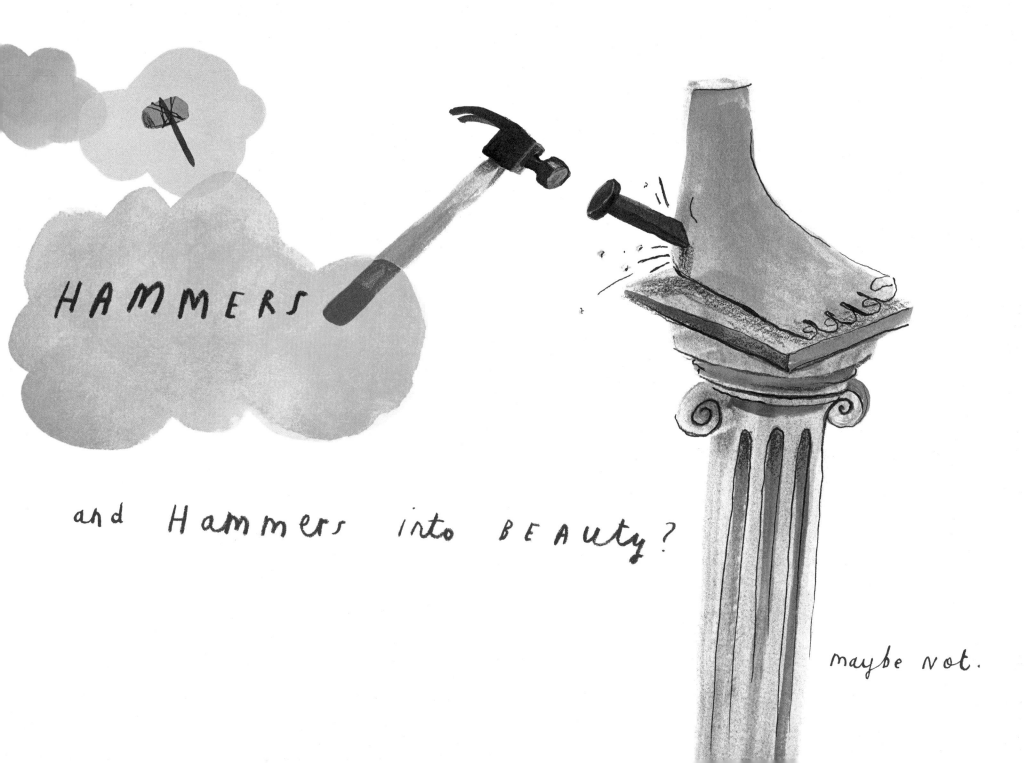

HAMMERS

and Hammers into BEAUTY?

maybe not.

ALRIGHT...

WHERE

SO...

DO WE GO FROM HERE ?

PERHAPS TO A PLACE
where WE Find NEW WAYs of USING
the OLD WAYS:
The HEAT From the STARS

the MOVEMENT of AIR

and WATER

USing WHAT WE FIND NEAR US to
MAKE with THE FUTURE in MIND

FOR PURPOSE

NOT POWER. For there is

AND LOVE,

ALREADY   POWER   Everywhere.

perhaps to a TIME

when WE NO LONGER NEED TO BURN

the SHIP WE ARE SAILing on

TO PROPEL US ...

when WE NO LONGer NEED A 'THEM'

so   WE   can   be...

'US'

AS WE are JUST WE .

And WHEREVER WE GO
WE ALL GO TOGETHER,

SO ALL of US MUST SEE
WE ARE NO longer JUST
PASSENGERS on This ship...

WE ARE ITS ONLY CREW,

WE EACH HAVE a part to PLAY.

WE MAY NOT BE COGS IN THE MACHINE
designed to be REPLACEable parts

BUT WE ARE TREES in the FOREST

NO one more important than ANY other

OK, WAIT... IF THAT'S ALL TRUE,

THEN HOW DO WE GET THERE?

By slowing down.

By creating
better stories.

BIGGER ONES

WHERE   WE   ALL   FIT

INSIDE the   SAME POWERFUL PLOT

IN WHICH WE THINK BEYOND OUR OWN

LIFETimes   BEYOND   OUR   CHILDREN'S...

AND THEIRS, And THEIrs,

and THEIRS, and Theirs, and theirs, and theirs, and theirs, and theirs

And it's OK to WALK There

(mostly)

For

There is WILD BEAUTY
in this LIFE on EARTH

And HOPE

wherever you look for it.

The Heart of It

When you dig
Deep enough,
By asking the why behind
The why
Enough times,
You come to a truth
At the heart of it;
That all people,
No matter who they are,
Where they are from,
or what they believe,
Just want the same things
A den
A pack
Position
And direction.

– Oliver Jeffers

Beginning Again: An Author's Note

So, why did I create this book?
And why am I writing an essay at the back of it?

To answer the second part first, I suppose in realising that the book itself has been difficult to define, it has prompted me to speak about the reasons why I made it in the first place.

What is this book exactly? I think it is a visual history, current review, and suggested trajectory for the human story. But what gives me the authority to confront such broad themes?

Nothing.

Except this: I believe there's no such thing as a foolish question. Asking someone to explain something I genuinely don't understand has never resulted in anyone thinking I'm a fool. Instead, it has enlightened both me and others who were too sheepish to ask themselves.

Over the last few years, I've started to wonder if my role in life is to ask the "foolish" questions loudly and fearlessly enough that we might clarify assumptions for the benefit of everyone. To attempt to distill things down to a simple enough point where they can be accessed, and be agreed upon, by anyone. To get to the centre of the spokes of the wheels of our interconnected lives, as it were.

This book is an attempt at doing just that.

With it, my inner worlds are finally intertwined. Until several years ago, my creativity had two distinct strands: visual stories mostly enjoyed by children and observational art mostly enjoyed by adults. But these different creative veins began to come together with the arrival of my son, Harland, in 2015, when what started as a letter to him about what it means to be a human alive in the 21st century eventually became the book *Here We Are: Notes for Living on Planet Earth*. All around me the world suddenly seemed bleaker and angrier than before. It was hard to tell whether it happened quite suddenly or whether I was just noticing from the perspective of being a first-time parent. And so, with that book for my son, I tried to counter it by showing him the simple truths that make up the beauty of life on Earth.

The first and most obvious lesson I learned from becoming a father came during the creation of *Here We Are*. It occurred to me that my newborn son, like all fresh arrivals, knew nothing of the ways in which humanity governs itself and thus would need to be taught how to function in society. Over time, he would no doubt figure out his tastes and—despite the best efforts of his mother and me—would be exposed to prejudices, some of which he would take as his own. In other words, I learned the gravity of this truth: we all arrive here on Earth as unwritten stories.

At the time of his birth, the world around me *really did* seem to be unraveling, and I began speaking publicly about things I'd always quietly observed and been moved by, but had not yet outwardly verbalised. I did this partly so one day I would be able to look my son (and my daughter, Mari, who showed up two years later) in the eyes while saying I tried to do my bit in an unjust world, and also because I felt the need to question the motivations of the stories that dominate the world stage. To make sense of them somehow. Stories like the growing transparency of inequality, a rising number of global refugees, divisive politics, the consequences of overconsumption, the fear of being replaced by a robot, the disposability of capitalism, and the cause and impact of climate-related natural disasters. But rather than just pointing out what was wrong and adding to the ever-growing noise of anger reverberating around the planet, I tried to remain hopeful, see a deeper pattern, or at least suggest positive action. I grew to recognise that by giving visual voice to my thoughts, I helped other people find their voice too, which encouraged me to continue doing so.

This book is the culmination of that observation and optimism.

In the process of forcing myself to consider how I feel about these issues and expressing it, I started to find that my—at first forced—optimism had genuine roots. The more I considered these weighty issues, the more I realised that our collective future may likely *not* be headed toward the dysfunctional dystopia we fear and frequently hear about. Perhaps it's less that the world seems to be unraveling, and more that we are now suddenly, and really for the first time ever, aware of everything happening everywhere, simultaneously and instantaneously—all the problems that have always existed but were somewhat isolated to the space in which they were playing out, so much so that it's easy to forget the progress we *have* made. We are now in a time when we have medicine for almost all ills; when we can expect to efficiently travel anywhere on this ball *and to return*, all before a season changes; when humans can talk to other humans anywhere, at any time, with immediate access to all information (real and fake); and when, for the most part, we live predictively long enough so that entire industries can be born to include things like exercise clothes for the elderly and books for children.

This optimistic and privileged view is not to say that everything is going perfectly. Far from it. We are a ways away from resources being fairly distributed and society being equitable. Injustices abound, and all of them need to be addressed. There is still war, famine, and poverty, and not everyone has this same access to travel, education, or medication that is so deeply needed. The world is now reckoning with the overlapping layers of pain from the past, at a time when a dawning realisation that the hedonistic way of recent living for some is choking us all—that the party is now over, and we're fighting over the bill— has become clear.

And while there *is* much to be worried about, and it *is* easy to feel that civilisation is headed in the wrong direction, the idea that we are all doomed and the planet is broken doesn't sit well with me. In fact, it feels fatalistic to resign ourselves to that idea. We are better than that. We will do what we have always done, which is to adapt. We just need to do so faster. And together. This is a tough ask of a fragmented species distracted by the chaos of a 24-hour cycle of an industry selling bad news.

And while empathy fatigue is very real, it's also important to remember that the most urgent issues we as a society are wrestling with today are the same ones that only a generation ago were met with indifference. That we now recognise them and debate them, at the very least, seems to show we're taking slow but steady steps in the right direction, despite how many more steps we know we still have to take. One of the most important next steps yet to be taken is addressing our growing sense of division, for any of our future solutions that hold will depend on unity.

I grew up in the politically divided and violent city of Belfast, Northern Ireland: a place where two opposing communities became insular and defensive to the point that their own identities became dependent on the existence of an enemy. I know all too well the destructive patterns of thought that foster an "us" versus "them" mentality. "I don't know who I am, but I know who I'm not" has all too often spilt into violence. Cultures may have clashed for millennia—history suggests that's what we tend to do when we encounter a new group: define our collective identity by our common enemy. But now that all of the cultures from around the world (and their stories) are known to each other—in part thanks to this internet era—they are beginning to finally meet for the first time around the table and are all competing with each other in a new way: both for dominance at the loudest level and simple acknowledgment at the quietest. It's a loud and confusing conversation that needs a different sort of diplomatic and empathic resolution.

I was raised as a Northern Irish Catholic and have experienced much of the grace and advantage that comes from being born into the body I inhabit. I have benefitted from the stories written by, and for, people mostly like me. But I have also experienced what it is to come from a (indeed the original) British colony. For most of the 20th century, Northern Irish Catholics were treated as second-class citizens. But by the mid-1980s, when I was a child being shielded on one hand and educated on the other, the origin of all this conflict was lost on me. It had always seemed obvious that it was never a religious war, and by the mid-'90s, it wasn't clear it had resulted from a class struggle either. Perhaps partly because I'd been told a particular set of stories, partly because I'd been made to compare these stories with others, and partly because I hadn't been told an array of other stories at all, it appeared more like political terrorism, or gangsterism with good PR. It had become a clash of identity more than a human rights issue, but either way it was undeniably a volatile background for my formative years.

Coming of age in this defensive, somewhat restrictive environment, I felt a need to move away from the home I'd known toward a bigger hub. So in 2007 I moved to New York City, where having a Belfast accent seemed to be an asset rather than the hindrance it was in London back then. At first I was shocked and hurt that no one on the other side of the Atlantic seemed to really know or care about the politically divided and traumatically violent history of where I came from, but slowly I came to accept that reality—we are an unimportant, inconsequential part of the top left-hand corner of Europe, so why *would* people be aware? I am not up to speed on the details of the very real political struggles of, say, Venezuela. But when I learned that British and even Southern Irish expatriates in NYC were also broadly ignorant about our Northern Irish tribulations, I experienced a new sort of frustration. We were all alone, killing each other in a fight to be part of either a larger Irish or British identity, but once beyond our borders—even *just barely* beyond the few hundred square miles of our province—no one seemed to care. I wasn't sure what to do with that disheartening reality.

Until I started reading about astronauts.

There is a phenomenon known as the overview effect, where any human who has been far enough from the surface of Earth tends to have the same shift in their perception of humanity when they see our collective story from the distance of outer space. In the first days on board the International Space Station, astronauts take to pointing out their hometowns and cities, which shifts outward to their countries, then the rough shapes of the continents that represent "home." And, finally, after enough time looking out the other window, into the inky abyss of our Milky Way galaxy, they have a profound realisation: this one object, floating in the cathedral of space, is home.

I began researching astronauts when making *Here We Are* and immediately recognised the way they described looking at Earth from space was how I'd been talking about Northern Ireland from across the distance of the Atlantic Ocean—the tragic waste of energy and life that consumed the minds of many seemed so pointless and poignant from afar. With distance comes perspective.

The summer after my son was born, there was international concern with the growing violence back in Belfast. As I watched the news footage from New York and saw that, like when I was growing up, it was kids who were hijacking and burning buses, throwing petrol bombs, rioting with each other and with the police, I wondered what these teenagers truly knew of the nuance of an 800-year-old conflict. The reality is, probably not much. They'd simply inherited a story from their parents that was validated by their peers. They'd been told who to hate and so they hated. This, I told myself, was *not* the story I was going to tell my children about where they came from. And as an artist, it was perhaps my biggest epiphany that the most powerful thing we can do as civilised human beings is change the story. We can always, *always* change the story. We can reframe our context and motivation to look at things as if they were part of a different, more productive narrative. We can choose to make a pattern of sense out of events to be governed by things other than fear or hate, anger or indifference. We can change *our own* story.

People are all, simply, a collection of stories: those we are told, those we tell, and those told about us. People become the stories they believe.

After 16 years in New York City, my wife, Suzanne, and I—with our two children in tow—found ourselves back in Northern Ireland. I ran away from Belfast years earlier because I was not interested in the stories we were telling about who we were. I did not like the value system of how someone was judged. I did not want to be where free thinking and ambition were seen as negatives. But in returning home to Belfast, after almost two decades away, I came to appreciate two things I'd previously missed—the value of family (and open green space) and the way in which Northern Ireland's revenge-identity politics echo in various ways across the world's conflicts. The Nobel Prize–winning poet Seamus Heaney (who was born and grew up but a few fields away from my mother) said near the end of his life, "The world is becoming one big Ulster," referring to the ancient province of Ireland that is now mostly Northern Ireland.

I left Northern Ireland thinking, *No one will ever understand our weird internal conflicts. I don't need to be a part of this anchor. I see bigger, more beautiful things about life on Earth, and I choose to pursue those.* But—having been in New York City for the brutal 2016 election cycle and the ensuing emotional upheaval, and then watching the even more brutal 2020 election cycle from across the ocean—it seemed that in America, revenge politics was coming to dominate personal thinking. If "they" think it's right, it must be wrong, whoever "they" may be. In Belfast, I was able to consider where several generations of divisive thinking gets you. Not far, if anywhere. Here, in Northern Ireland, we were *still* trying to justify our past. Our attention was (and is) consumed by this battle of stories, in a way that continues to hamper our future. People were, and still are, continually going against their own best interests trying to prove they are right. That their story is right.

I noticed that I'd started taking much of my feelings on geopolitics from watching Suzanne be a mother. I learned, watching her, that you'll never get someone to change their mind by telling them they are wrong. Your stance may seem true and obvious to you, but emotionally, this aggressive mode of communication doesn't work. It never has and it never will. It merely manifests a defensive mentality. Adults just seem to hold on to being defensive much longer than children do.

When, on returning to Belfast, I saw a paramilitary mural depicting two masked gunmen accompanying the slogan WE DESERVE THE FUNDAMENTAL RIGHT, IF ATTACKED, TO DEFEND OURSELVES, I considered it in a new light. This was a global problem, not just a local one, where everyone, everywhere, feels attacked. When I ask people "What kind of a world do you want?" I have noticed they tend to answer with what they *don't* want rather than trying to imagine what their ideal future world might look like and how they might get there. They are answering a positive question with aggressive defence. Certainly, there are global conflicts all over the world where people are in physical danger. But why do those of us who are not in such circumstances feel so constantly threatened by and alienated from each other? Is this sense of being under attack warranted? If not, where does it come from? Maybe it's simply easier to blame something with a face than to blame an abstract concept like when your reality turns out to be different from the story you were promised.

I have traveled all over the world on book tours. I've been to dozens of countries, and almost all fifty United States; I have met many people from all backgrounds, belief systems, and political leanings. I very much believe the vast majority of people on Earth are good people—when it comes down to it, on an individual level we tend to be naturally considerate, generous, and empathic. I suppose that shifts when we start to think as groups, about groups. But we are built to help each other and work together. Almost all the people I've met on the road are good people. I've never met anyone who actually *wanted* to be disliked, even among the people who'd often be considered assholes. They, too, just wanted a better life for themselves. For their children.

But what does that mean? What is a better life?

These days, instead of asking people what they want, the question I ask is, "How do you want to feel?"

After we feel safe, we all just want to feel that we fit in, that we belong. We want to matter. And growing numbers of people despair that they don't. That they have instead been forgotten, are unimportant, left out of the collective story of modern society.

In a chance encounter with an old lady waiting to cross the road in Belfast during the pandemic, in the days before the global lockdown took effect, I asked if she thought we were in for a long road. "Yes," she responded. "I was around during the [Second World] War, and back then everyone tried to see how they could help, but look around, everyone today just tries to see what they can get away with. We aren't getting out of this quickly because no one is going to cooperate." The simplicity of her words struck me. They were not untrue. When did this fissure begin? How did we go from community to individual? From "we" to "me"?

Was it a defense mechanism applied by people protecting themselves against the feeling that they didn't matter, in a world where "growth" is the measuring stick of success?

I wonder if we've been using the wrong measuring stick.

And in an age where we have been taught to think of ourselves first—that we as individuals are all important—it is understandable that when our personal stories seem left to the wayside, we feel defeated or angered. What we need to understand, though, is that "it's not all about me." To build a better future, we need to think toward the collective, what might work communally. But how do we change how we're taught to think?

Another valuable observation I've gathered from watching Suzanne mother is the power of telling a better story. Issues don't necessarily need to be resolved before people move on. There doesn't need to be a conclusion or a winner.

Around the world, there is a growing trend toward nationalism, where disparate groups are brought together behind a similar story. Old stories are forgotten in the face of a bigger, seemingly more important one. The stories that bind these groups tend to be hateful ones, offering something or someone to blame rather than a sense of purpose. But it works because these new stories include the people they are being told to. They are giving people who feel forgotten a sense of purpose, however shallow.

But there must be a better way. A more powerful story that binds, rather than tears, the fabric of society. I've always believed the most powerful human emotion is not hate, not fear, not even love, but hope. Hope separates us from other animals, as it requires imagination about an unwritten future. The ink on the next few hastily written lines of that untold story of the world we might live in is barely dry, and we are already wary of its premise.

The antiquated stories, the old ones we've told for centuries of the rules about how we conduct ourselves that we are still intent on justifying, have little place in the world we are working toward. What future collective story would we rather compose? Certainly one that further builds on and encourages those already written, strong in their foundations of hope and inclusion. And creating these new stories, these new systems that work for everybody, is an enormous undertaking. It will require the largest army of people ever assembled at a time when an enormous number of people feel lost, without cause or purpose. It is time we bring these two groups together. To ring the bell for a much-needed global renovation. How, though, do we begin?

In 2022, I attended a climate conference in Scotland, where I was one of the only artists in attendance, amid scientists, delegates, and business leaders. I gave a breakout workshop where thirty or so attendees helped me make a mural. For many involved, it was the first time they'd picked up a paintbrush in decades. I got asked multiple times throughout the three-day conference "How can I take what you do to make what I do look better?" They were asking the wrong question of art. They saw art as decoration. But that's not what art is. Art is *not* the icing on the cake. It is not even the cake. It is the table on which the cake sits.

Art's purpose is to imperceptibly shift the ground under people's feet. Science, technology, engineering and math are *how* we do things. Art is *why* we do them.

Stories may be the most important pillar of art.

We undervalue art in modern education. We learn to read an image, a face, a room before we learn how to read a word or to count, yet art is mostly seen as something to distract and entertain more than anything else. As we try to remake the world, education is one of the many systems, as countless educators are painfully aware of, that needs urgently to be rebuilt. My father, a lifelong educator, always pointed out that knowing a lot of facts doesn't prove intelligence. It just proves you've got a good memory. True intelligence, my dad always suggested, is curiosity and imagination. And those are two skills people have in abundance. We're just not often prompted to use them. How would we redesign education if it were based around producing future contributing members of a shifting society? There are better brains than mine deeply at work on this endeavour. A better question is to ask, then, is why are they meeting so much resistance? The old rules run deep, and their roots are hard to pull from our earth.

The next generation of education should champion curiosity and imagination. Empathy and joy. Reward inclusive innovation that can help civilisation thrive in a changing climate. All of which will help in reframing our bigger story, one told in harmony, that can be used to address our bigger problems.

As an example, for all the problems we face in a rapidly changing environment growing hostile to life, there are solutions. We just have yet to rally around the same stories that will motivate us to implement them. We don't have a climate problem so much as we have a people problem—a cacophony of fractured stories that suit the teller, not the told, further obscuring any sense of shared destination. A puzzle,

in other words, that seems more solvable than controlling the weather. Imagine a scenario where all of us, suddenly and clearly, become energised by a much better story. One that aims toward a flourishing future, instead of being driven by being "right" or by what we can simply just get away with in our own individual lifetimes. Aside from safeguarding the future of civilisation, it might make the brief time we each get being alive on Earth all the more beautiful and joyful too.

A simple, deep, and accessible place to begin shifting these disjointed motivations we find scattered across the people of our planet might be to make a conscious effort to replace "right" and "wrong" in the context of any conflict or debate with "better" and "worse." It's not hard to see how a simple shift in perception, in an internal narrative, can change everything.

When the *Apollo 8* astronauts turned and looked at Earth as they rounded the moon, the first humans to ever see the entirety of our world as one single object, they couldn't work out what part of Earth they were looking at. It took them longer than they'd have expected to realise it was the horn of Africa. Because it was *sideways*. We have been conditioned to think of the map with north at the top and south at the bottom, but this is a made-up construction. In reality there is no up or down to our planet. This is just a system we created for ourselves. A story.

To put this perspective shift into practice again, scientifically speaking, we are at the outer edge of a small galaxy, far from the brightest points of our cosmos. But instead of saying we are in a cold and lonely part of space, we could reasonably find comfort in this alternative: if this is the only place where life exists, then we are in the middle of the least lonely place in the universe.

Here, in the social heart of the cosmos, I hope this book inspires you to change the way you act, speak, and more importantly, the way you *think* about your role in an unknown future—a story that has yet to be told, a story we must all tell, together.

Oliver Jeffers is an artist and author from Belfast, Northern Ireland, who divides his time between there and Brooklyn, New York, where he lived for 16 years. Known for his picture books for children, fine art for adults, and public art sculptures for both, Oliver has been a #1 *New York Times* bestseller multiple times, and his books have sold more than 15 million copies and been translated into over 50 languages. He is the recipient of numerous awards, including a *New York Times* Best Illustrated Children's Books Award, a BolognaRagazzi Award, an Irish Book Award, a United Kingdom Literary Association Book Award, *TIME* magazine's Book of the Year, a BAFTA for the adaptation of *Lost and Found*, and two Emmy Awards for the Apple TV adaptation of *Here We Are: Notes for Living on Planet Earth*. He also received an MBE for Services to the Arts from her late Majesty Queen Elizabeth II.

Photograph © Yasmina Cowan

PHILOMEL
An imprint of Penguin Random House LLC, New York

First published in the United Kingdom by HarperCollins Children's Books, 2023
First published in the United States of America by Philomel,
an imprint of Penguin Random House LLC, 2023

Visit us online at PenguinRandomHouse.com.

Library of Congress Cataloging-in-Publication Data is available.

Manufactured in China

ISBN 9780593621554

10 9 8 7 6 5 4 3 2 1

TOPL

Edited by Jill Santopolo
Design by Rory Jeffers
Text font by Oliver Jeffers

This book is a work of fiction. Any references to historical events, real people,
or real places are used fictitiously. Other names, characters, places, and events are
products of the author's imagination, and any resemblance to actual
events or places or persons, living or dead, is entirely coincidental.

The art for this book was made using Holbein matte acrylic, gouache paint,
and coloured pencil on Arches hot press paper.

Thank You
Suzanne Jeffers, Fruzsi Czech, Rory Jeffers, Philippa Jordan, Emma Miller,
Sam Fisher, Jill Santopolo, Ellice Lee, Aaron Ruff, Gabe Benzur, Alice Blacker,
Val Brathwaite, Geraldine Stroud, Paul Moreton, David Pearson, Chris Anderson,
Debbie Millman, Mac Premo, Duke Riley, Lucien Zayan, Katie Rosenbaum, Todd
Rosenbaum, Steve Dembitzer, Harland Jeffers, Mari Jeffers, Paul Jeffers, Aaron Ruff,
Stefan Sagmeister, Lindsay Todd, Erin Allweiss, Jen Loja, Shanta Newlin, Helen
MacKenzie Smith and Alec Samways.